MW00381099

THE ORIGINAL PEER SUPPORT RECOVERY & COPING SKILLS WORKBOOK & CURRICULUM

Gregorio Lewis

Better Days Recovery Press

The Original Peer Support Recovery & Coping Skills Workbook & Curriculum
First Edition © 2022 by Craig Lewis. All Rights Reserved.
ISBN: 978-1-4357-65719

Copying and distributing portions of this book without citing the source is a violation of copyright. Copying and distributing this book in part or in its entirety is a violation of copyright, with the exceptions listed above. Sale of materials from this work without permission is not permitted.

Published by Better Days Recovery Press
survivingtheimpossible@gmail.com
www.sanityisafulltimejob.org

Copy edited by Dan Gardner
Additional editing by Chris Mellen
Production edited by Soumen Dutta
Photo by Café Gitano
Cover design by Robert Eaton

Contents

Acknowledgments

I give thanks to all who have honored me in this life. I sometimes struggle with staying alive. I believe in recovery. I am a realist. Life can be as unfair and unjust as it can be beautiful and fulfilling. Sometimes it feels like it would be easier to walk away. This book exists because I still believe in trying my best to be okay, and I still believe that life is worth living.

This book exists because I choose to try to heal and learn how to cope better so that I could perhaps live a peaceful, stable and happy life. I give thanks to you, the person who is holding this book in your hands. It is because of you that this book exists. Thank you for helping me exist. Not to simply stay alive, yet magnificently; to truly live.

INTRODUCTION

Raw Old School Back to Basics - that's this book.

At some point, people walking the recovery path look in the mirror and dislike what they see.

It is not funny, but as we say in colloquial American English, it's funny…

It's funny that people can work so hard and get better and then collapse again.

Is it funny or is it not funny?

This depends on your appreciation for humor as much as your willingness to surrender.

I first heard the word "recovery" in the mental health context in 2006. On the very same day, I first heard the words "Peer Specialist".

I've walked the recovery path for 16 years.

It's funny how sometimes the more things change; the more things change.

There ain't no shame in the recovery game; you have to be in it to win it.

You know that fear that you have inside: you don't want anyone to know that you are falling to pieces and hanging on by a thread. I had the distinct pleasure of living that private concern and have it become my public reality.

That is why I keep describing my experiences as funny.

Nobody wants to be the recovery superstar who falls from grace, never to return to stability.

It is funny that we recovery educators so emphatically emphasize the truth that recovery is a non-linear journey. It is funny for me because I get to be the living breathing evidence that what we teach and preach is true.

If you are saying to yourself, "Hey, haven't I seen this before?" The answer is yes, sort of.

The pages in this book were written between 2007-2011, partially as part of my internship to become a Certified Peer Specialist, and then as part of the Better Days support group.

Beginning in 2013, the peer specialist authored, Better Days Mental Health Recovery Workbook became an unexpected do-it-yourself, self-published hit, with over 10,000 copies in print.

The book is the second Better Days Mental Health Recovery Workbook.

So, choose to walk your talk and do the work. No matter what happens, keep doing it and keep improving yourself because your life will improve.

Gregorio Lewis
June 18, 2022
México

FOREWORD

I will never forget the moment I met Mr. Craig Lewis. I was sitting outside my friend's house, in my car, cruising the Facebook newsfeed in a frenzy. I was on the prowl, looking, searching for something. Like most of us on social media, we aren't always looking for something specific.

Sometimes, we are gazing at our screens, waiting for that "Oh, wow!" moment to strike when we stumble on to a juicy piece of celebrity gossip, news, or the following weight-loss strategy to shed a few pounds before the next social meetup.

Let me provide a little more context—the beginning of COVID. Flight restrictions were beginning to mount, and no one knew what was next. I am in the health profession, specifically mental health. So, when the news was starting to emerge about COVID on the Facebook Newsfeed, I watched and hoped to learn what I could do about this frightening new threat to my mental peace.

Like most of us, I hope to learn more about my craft. As a self-proclaimed 'Prosumer,' I aim to produce information on my blog Mental Health Affairs, every day. I also consume information, ideas, and concepts to treat my diagnosis of Schizophrenia, hoping to heal further and recover.

So, when I stumbled on to a friend of a friend's 'share,' from a Mr. Craig Lewis, talking about traveling back to Mexico on an airplane and a litany of replies, warm wishes, and self-statements about his mental health, my focus was firmly fixed on the thread in front of me.

That's when I began reading about Mr. Craig Lewis. Outside my friend's house, still parked, but now getting texts from my friend inquiring about why I was still outside, parked on my phone on Facebook. "I'll be inside soon," I texted my friend. As I continued reading Craig's feed, looking back on his timeline, I knew it would be a while until this first encounter was over.

Soon, I found myself sending Craig a direct message. Before I knew it, we were talking on an audio call. A little later, I walked into my friend's house, gesturing to my phone, signaling I was on a call with someone important. That was over three years ago.

Three years later, I serendipitously find myself writing this Foreword to Craig's most crucial literary creation yet, The Original Peer Support Recovery and Coping Skills Workbook & Curriculum. Over the last three years, I have had the tremendous pleasure of learning about Craig's literary works. I have read and studied all of them from the vantage point of the Prosumer.

I can confidently say how versatile Mr. Craig Lewis's books are to the reader in their application and contribution to the existing Mental Health discourse, Mr. Craig Lewis's books raise the bar that much higher for every author that walks in his footsteps on the recovery literature scene.

The Original Peer Support Recovery and Coping Skills Workbook & Curriculum challenge its readers with worksheets, exercises, and self-empowering statements to help readers reframe, rethink, and motivate again and again as the book unfolds. These exercises are as powerful as they are authentic. We are learning from the Recovery guru himself, who used and practiced these tools himself in his recovery, a path the author is open and transparent.

Mr. Craig Lewis's book needs to sit on the shelves of clubhouses and community rooms for people to access at their disposal. The Original Peer Support Recovery and Coping Skills Workbook & Curriculum belong in day treatment programs everywhere. Mr. Lewis's book should be required reading for patients embarking upon discharge from inpatient and partial hospitals needing recovery-oriented skills for living in the community.

As a mental health therapist, I sometimes struggle to find accessible and relatable material to complete in sessions with my patients and exercises for homework assignments in between sessions. The Original Peer Support Recovery and Coping Skills Workbook & Curriculum offer a robust and plentiful assortment of activities. Even the most seasoned mental health worker will never go without as long as they have a copy.

If you are looking for high-tech, sugar-coated rhetoric that is overpriced and, quite frankly, dated, look elsewhere. Craig Lewis, in his writing, lifestyle, and connectedness to the real struggle of people living with mental health issues, has ushered in a 'Post-Pat Deegan' era in recovery rhetoric.

Mr. Lewis has gone beyond my wildest expectations with The Original Peer Support Recovery and Coping Skills Workbook & Curriculum. I am confident that when you pick this book up and begin reading, you, the reader, and my words here will be on the same page.

Max E. Guttman, LCSW (Licensed Clinical Social Worker)
Website: mentalhealthaffairs.blog
Email: maxwellguttman@gmail.com
Pseudonym: J. PETERS

Hope

On some days, hope is all I have.

I will fight to live a better life because I want to be happy and successful and because I deserve it.

No one else can tell me that I can't have a better life in which I am happy and healthy.

We decide if we want to live a good and healthy life.

We must reject negative and unhelpful thinking.

Each of us has the power within us to change for the better.

Each of us has the responsibility to work as hard as we can to improve our lives.

We are in control of our lives. Allow yourself to be in control of your life.

We will rise above stigma and be all that we can be.

It will be your victory.

Hope WORKSHEET

1.   What are five things that I am proud of in my life?

2.   What are five things that I most want to improve in my life?

3.   Recovery is   .

Hope WORKSHEET

Doing What's Right

I am a person who sometimes experiences extreme feelings.

These feelings cause me to feel excellent and sometimes not so good.

I struggle with knowing what to do with my feelings when they feel so strong.

Sometimes I react to things I experience in exaggerated ways.

Often, when I am feeling intense emotions, this happens.

I must never forget that I am a human being.

My life will continue moving forward even if I overreact at times.

We can learn from this and find some peace in our lives.

Doing What's Right WORKSHEET

1.   List three situations in your life that cause you to experience strong emotions?

2.   Give one example where you did something positive for yourself even though it was hard to do.

3.   List three experiences that make you feel happy.

Facing Life Head On

Every single day, we are confronted with difficult dilemmas and issues that we must face. Sometimes these decisions can have a serious impact on our lives and how we live. I recently had to make a very quick decision to have surgery. I only had a few minutes to make my decision and there were only three days until I would actually be having the surgery. I had to weigh the benefits of jumping into the deep end of a pool head first and completely rearranging my life for the next two weeks with very little time to do so.

I also had to figure out how my life would be impacted if I waited two months to have the surgery during my semester at school and also the emotional impact that waiting would have on me. There were many factors to consider including financial issues, having to cancel and reschedule everything in my life for the period of two weeks and sacrificing my personal free time while on vacation from school and work. As it turned out, I made a great decision.

It certainly was not easy to make this decision and deal with the consequences. At the end of the day, what I found was that the fact that I was in recovery and doing well and stable allowed me to accept this unexpected surgery. I simply had to be able to adapt to it and make it work for me. Now I am on top of the world and my health is much better off as well.

Long live Recovery.

Facing Life Head On WORKSHEET

1. Name a situation in which you were faced with a difficult decision. What did you decide to do and how did the situation turn out for you?

2. Name a difficult situation that you think you will have to deal with in the future, and how you think would be the best way to deal with it?

3. I believe in Recovery because

Making Choices

Every day, we make dozens of choices. We choose what clothes we wear, whether or not we will take a shower, what we will eat, and we choose how messy or clean our living space is. I struggle with keeping my apartment clean and organized. This has been a struggle for me for many, many years.

Today my apartment is a mess and I don't like it. I feel bad living with dishes piled up in the sink and clutter everywhere. I want to make things better yet I don't know how. I try to clean and organize and the clutter and mess always returns.

Today I took a step forward and I called a woman who specializes in helping people by teaching better ways of organizing their living space. It costs money, but it is worth it. Also, today I commit to cleaning all the rooms in my apartment on different days each and every week.

I am making a choice to improve my life. This choice, for me, is recovery.

Making Choices WORKSHEET

1.   One thing that I can do to improve my life is:

2.   One issue in my life that I think I could make better choices about is;

3.   During this past week, the best choice that I have made for myself was:

Self-Advocacy

Throughout much of my life, I can remember that I have had many times that I needed someone to help me and speak up on my behalf. I had so many needs that were not addressed. Even to this day, I am aware of the extreme damage that has been done to me after years of not having my needs met. As a teenager growing up in many unnatural situations, no one spoke up and advocated for my personal and intimate needs. I was just another troubled teenager living in a group home.

One thing that I wish I learned those many years ago was the act of self-advocacy. After living through some extremely dreadful and horrendous life situations, I have learned how to better advocate for myself. Most everything that I have in my life, I have as a result of my self-advocacy.

When we are able to effectively speak up about our needs, then our lives will be better. Self-advocacy is our tool – Use it!

Self-Advocacy WORKSHEET

1.   Give one example of a time in which you advocated for your needs?

2.   What is one example where you did not speak up in order to have your needs met and what would you do differently next time?

3.   What do the words "self-advocacy" mean to you?

Perspective

It never fails: warm, windy days bring my mind to a place where I can smile, feel gentle, and relax. There is something about warm, windy days that brings me to a true and happy place.

For some people, it may be the smell of freshly baked brownies that brings alive those good feelings inside. Perhaps for others, it may be the smell of the ocean or the smell of a wood stove. Other people might feel moved by a certain song, movie, or poem.

In our lives, we must find positive ways to connect with what naturally makes us feel good. We know that there are positive and healthy things in this world that help us feel better and live happier lives. The challenge is to identify what these positive and healthy things are and find ways to connect with them when we are struggling.

Ultimately, it is up to each and every one of us to figure out positive and healthy ways to live and feel better. When we are struggling, we can redirect our train of thought to think about the wonderful, beautiful, and good things in our lives and in this world and, thus, find our Better Days.

When we willingly improve our perspective, we will feel better.

Perspective WORKSHEET

1.   When I am struggling the #1 thing that can help me feel better is?

2.   Please share an example of something that brings you joy.

3.   Something cool about me that most people don't know is?

Pain Will Pass

On some days, I feel as if I am carrying a one thousand pound weight on my back. On some days, I feel depression, fear, loneliness, grief, and helplessness.

I acknowledge that I do not always know what to do when it comes to dealing with the intensities that I face, sometimes daily, in my life.

Sometimes, upsetting things can happen in our lives that are difficult to make better.

One thing that I do know is that the pain and hurt will pass. The pain and hurt that often feels so overwhelming; it will pass and I will grow from my experiences.

We will learn better ways to have Better Days regardless of how much we may struggle from one day to the next.

Pain Will Pass WORKSHEET

1. What are three positive things that we can learn from our experiences with experiencing emotional pain?

2. When you feel overwhelmed, in what ways do you seek help (who do you call, ask for support, etc)?

3. What is one new thing that might help you consider trying to cope with and heal from the pain you experience?

Being Responsible to Yourself

In order to gain and maintain our recovery, we must take responsibility for ourselves, our lives and our actions. What is responsibility and why is being responsible crucial to having our positive mental health?

There have been times where I have made some very poor choices in my life. The best thing that I could do is try and learn from my mistakes. If I am able to acknowledge that the choices I make can play a role in how well I am doing on any given day, then, I have found a major tool for experiencing lasting wellness.

No one besides myself can make me change for the better. Our life experiences have taught us some difficult lessons so let us all learn from these lessons and grow into our happier, healthy and better lives.

Better Days are absolutely on the way, and are without a doubt, here to stay.

Being Responsible to Yourself

Being Responsible to Yourself WORKSHEET

1.   List three things in your life that you want to improve?

2.   List the three biggest obstacles that are in the way of you having a happier and healthier life.

3.   If I want to live a happier and healthier life, what are three things I can do today to make this happen?

Being Responsible to Yourself WORKSHEET

Positive Risk

This weekend, I took a step forward in my recovery. I took a positive risk. I was scared and nervous, however, I stood up to my feelings and I succeeded.

It is never easy having to take a chance. Recovery is such a precious thing. I know that in order to live a better quality life, I must take some chances. I am talking about taking a positive risk. This is how I move forward.

I must give myself the chance to heal; to get better.

No one will do it for me; Only I can do it for myself.

Sometimes we have to invest in our better future, Better Day by Better Day by Better Day.

Positive Risk WORKSHEET

1.   What do you do to move forward after something intense and upsetting happens in your life?

2.   What is a positive risk that you have taken recently?

3.   What is one thing you would like to improve about your life and how you live it?

Improvements

Although I am doing very well, there are many things about my life that I want to improve. We can always make improvements toward bettering the quality of our lives. For me, I need to be more social, go to bed earlier, organize my room better and slack off less when it comes to doing my chores and my homework.

What are some things about your life that you would like to, or need to, improve?

It is healthy to want to be healthier and happier. We deserve to live a good quality life making one improvement at a time.

Improvements WORKSHEET

1.   List three improvements that you would like to make in your life?

2.   List one reason why it is important to you to improve your life?

3.   List something that you would like to improve in your life and two ideas that you can consider attempting to make your better life a reality.

When Good Things Happen

I can't believe it.

I have experienced so much pain, hurt and difficulty in my life that I sometimes become unable to accept the good things when they happen.

This is an honest reaction to a very tough life.

I have put in a lot of hard work to make improvements in my life and to be in recovery.

Recovery is a constant daily process that we must always put our effort toward in order to live the better life we want and to have Better Days.

Today, thankfully, several good things happened.

It was unexpected. However, these good things are a testament to all of my effort, hard work and dedication that I have put toward my recovery and living a better life.

Sometimes good things happen and we need to accept, acknowledge and celebrate these good things.

Why, you ask? Because we are worth it!

When Good Things Happen WORKSHEET

1.   The best part of being in recovery is?

2.   The most difficult part of being in recovery is?

3.   When I am upset the best thing I can do to take care of myself is?

Overcoming Dread

Sometimes in our lives we face dreadful situations.

Sometimes circumstances are so terrible and unmanageable that we feel helpless.

Many people living with the impact of trauma seem to face a disproportionate amount of these terrible situations.

However, we are often expected to handle these dreadful situations as if they were no big deal.

The truth is that we are not machines or robots and we have real feelings of fear, hurt and pain.

We often face these dreadful situations head on and battle through them like warriors.

We will benefit by remembering that we have made it this far in our lives and struggles - we have overcome so much.

If we want to live happier and healthier lives and experience better days, we need to be gentle to ourselves and remind ourselves that we are doing the best we can.

Overcoming Dread WORKSHEET

1.　　When we are faced with a dreadful situation, what are three things that we can do to help ourselves cope in a healthy way?

2.　　Give one example of how you successfully managed a dreadful situation.

3.　　Do you believe that you are worthy of living a happier and healthier life? Why?

Physical Health Challenges

When I woke up on Monday, I showered and got ready for work.

I knew quickly I was not feeling very well. I had a terrible stomach ache and was disoriented.

I called in sick to work and slept for the rest of the day and for much of Tuesday.

I could not eat much of anything and I was miserable.

I desperately wanted to go to work and live my busy and active life.

Instead, I was stuck in bed and sick – a total letdown.

Now it is Wednesday and I am thankfully feeling much better. I am now back at work and again living my active life.

I really did not like being sick. Maybe, I need some extra time to rest so I could be better prepared and ready to face my life and the world.

Perhaps spending extra time in bed and at home doing very little will be helpful for my wellness and recovery.

Well, that is the way I view my life – things happen for a reason.

Today I am happy, content and healthy and raring to go.

I am feeling much better today and ready to face the world more than I was last week.

My suffering has value and I intend to learn from it and continue to grow.

Physical Health Challenges WORKSHEET

1. Give an example of a helpful lesson you've learned as a result of hardship and struggle.

2. When you are feeling physically unhealthy– what are three things that others can do to help you feel better?

3. In your moment of struggle, are you able to consider that the next day your life may be easier to manage, happier and less stressful?

Getting Back on Track

These past few weeks have been very difficult for me.

I have not been doing well.

I know what it is that triggered me.

There is very little that I can do about it. What I can do is take steps to improve myself, work on strengthening my coping skills and move forward.

One thing that I can do is focus on getting myself back on track toward being healthy and happy.

I have suffered enough and I want my life back.

I choose how I react to things in my life and I decide if I want to move forward.

I can take positive steps to feel emotional and mental relief and I can and I will succeed at this.

I will work hard for my better days and I will achieve my goals.

We can all take steps toward achieving our goals!

It will be your victory!

Getting Back on Track

Getting Back on Track WORKSHEET

1.   List three things that you can do to get back on track when you are struggling.

2.   Name one thing that you struggle with and two ways in which you can effectively deal with it.

3.   In your opinion, is it possible to gain more control over how we react to the difficult things that we face in our lives?

Dealing with Conflict

The majority of the conflicts that I have had with other people may have been avoidable.

The negative impact of these conflicts has caused me much pain and hurt.

This pain and hurt may have been avoidable.

How many times have I allowed myself to be hurt as a result of being unable to walk away from conflict?

How many times have I suffered needlessly after having been triggered?

If I can teach myself to walk away from difficult conversations or situations, I will have a better chance at achieving my goals and dreams.

If I want to live a happier life and a healthier life, I can learn to respond in a different way to those triggers.

Better Days are on the way and Better Days are here to stay.

Dealing with Conflict **WORKSHEET**

1.   In what ways do the conflicts I have with others negatively impact my life?

2.   Give one example of a conflict that you've had and one way you think you could have dealt with it better?

3.   In order to live the live I want, I need to:

Dealing with Conflict: Trusting Others

In my life, I have experienced a great deal of conflict. At times, I have struggled with knowing which people I can get the most helpful support from. This is an issue of trust. Let's talk about what trust is and how having a trustworthy confidant important to your recovery: Having a safe person who you can trust to help you is important. Having that person will help you feel less alone in your struggle.

As people in recovery, our lives present countless opportunities for us to develop trust in others and to learn to trust ourselves. We can create Better Days, one trusting moment at a time because we do not need to be alone in our struggle.

Dealing with Conflict: Trusting Others

1. List the names of three people who you can trust if you are having an intense challenge.

2. How do you manage a tough situation when you don't have someone to talk to for support?

3. Why is being able to trust others important to your recovery?

Inspiration

What is inspiration? What does it mean to be inspired?

As a person who is a peer supporter, I come in contact with many people who may be struggling yet want to make things better.

These individuals might benefit from some words of encouragement or an expression of mutual support and understanding.

The people I find inspiring are the ones who are trying hard to improve their lives.

These people make me want to develop and facilitate the Better Days group every week.

This is because I feel inspired by being part of this group.

I want to work hard to improve my life.

Sharing with others who are also trying to make their lives better is inspiring.

Finding your inspiration is a vital component to recovery and wellness.

When we are able to recognize what it is that inspires us to live better lives, we then are better able to live those lives.

Inspiration WORKSHEET

1. List three things in your life that inspire you.

2. Give an example of when you think that you inspired another person.

3. This workbook inspires me to

No More Crash and Burn

Dealing with trauma and mental health challenges can be incredibly tough. Sometimes how we are impacted can really make us feel terrible. I know how it feels when the whole world seems to be caving in on me.

I often feel I don't even know what I am doing when it comes to my life and my recovery.

Nevertheless, I work hard to keep myself together when I am not doing well and I have found that my recovery has been holding my hand tightly during my struggles.

What happens is my choice.

My choice is to not crash and burn.

I instead wish to focus on being healthy and productive.

I fell in love with life again as the birds sang beautifully outside my window.

No More Crash and Burn WORKSHEET

1.   What are three things that you can do to work toward feeling better when you are struggling?

2.   When the world feels like it is caving in on you, what options do you have to make things better?

3.   What are three things that happen with you or in your life that tell you that you are doing well?

Experiencing Recovery

Today may be the beginning of the beginning of my being well. I must be realistic; it is absolutely possible that I might be feeling better as of today.

Things in my life could be a lot worse. I have suffered and my suffering has been a great teacher. If there is a lesson out there to be taught, I want to learn it. I suspect that I may have been well these past several weeks and just not have known it.

Perhaps this was a necessary part of experiencing recovery. If I am hurting, yet stay on track, – that is recovery. If you are struggling or in despair and you continue to work hard to keep yourself together, – is recovery. If we make it through each hard day and wake up the next, – that is recovery. If I want to live more than I want to die, that is recovery.

Experiencing Recovery WORKSHEET

1.   What does it mean to you to experience recovery?

2.   In what ways do you know that you are doing well?

3.   How does this coping skills guidebook help you improve the quality of your life?

Accepting Your Life

Life happens.

Life will go on whether things have been fair or not.

Life will go on if you have made a big mistake.

Life will go on if you win a million dollars.

Life will go on no matter what.

Life will go on if you break your arm.

Life will go on if you have to have surgery.

Life will go on if you have a financial crisis.

Life will go on. Your life will continue.

We must accept that life will happen and sometimes there is nothing that we can do about it. If we suffer pain, loneliness, regret, embarrassment or any other difficult feeling we must accept our life. We must accept our life and we must accept our reality. We must also accept that each and every one of us has the power within to make a Better Day for ourselves no matter what the circumstances that we find ourselves in.

Life will go on no matter what.

I know that I will live my life fighting for that Better Day because I have to.

I have no other option. Better Days are on the way and Better Days are here to stay.

Accepting Your Life **WORKSHEET**

1.   What are three things that you feel are unfair about your life?

2.   In what three ways do you live your life in a hopeful way?

3.   What are three steps that you could take to make your life better today?